WORDS OF

Swami Vivekananda

Ramakrishna Mission Institute of Culture
Gol Park, Kolkata - 700 029

Published by

Swami Suparnananda
Secretary
Ramakrishna Mission Institute of Culture
Gol Park, Kolkata-700 029

First Edition : January, 1988 : 2,000
Twenty-first Impression : June 2016 : 10,000
Total Impression : 1,83,000

ISBN : 81-85843-25-2

Price : 25.00

Published on the Occasion of the 125th Birth
Anniversary of Swami Vivekananda

Printed at

Ramakrishna Mission Institute of Culture
Kolkata 700 029

FOREWORD

Unawares, Swami Vivekananda very often said things that startled his audience. He said them casually, carelessly, without any thought about the impact that they might produce. What he said might be simple truths, but it is these simple truths spoken with authority and coming spontaneously from a world teacher, that disturb you most. They remind you of your present limitations and of the great heights to which you might yet rise. They shake you to your roots, sweeping away all the depression you have allowed to accumulate over the years and releasing within you new sources of energy which carry you forward.

It is some of such utterances by Swami Vivekananda which Prof. Govinda Gopal Mukherjee, with the assistance of two research assistants, working under him, Madhabi Sinha and Parna Mukherjee, has picked up from among Swamiji's speeches and writings from *The Complete Works of Swami Vivekananda*, published by Advaita Ashrama, Mayavati which this little book presents to the readers. While reading the utterances the readers may experience the same kind of electric shock which Romain Rolland experienced when he first read Swamiji.

Swami Lokeswarananda

23 January 1988

INDIA'S DISCOVERY OF HERSELF

Swami Lokeswarananda

When Swami Vivekananda (1863-1902) returned to India after his first successful tour in the West, a disciple asked him why he had gone to the West. Indeed, that was a moot question. How much he had to pay for what many then regarded as a clear act of indiscretion! To give just one instance, his entry into the Dakshineswar temples was banned! But what was Swami Vivekananda's reply to the question? He said that he went to the West from a sheer of frustration. During his years as a wandering monk in India, he said he had seen many prominent people in this country. He had drawn their attention to the plight of the masses and bagged them to do something for them. They paid no heed to him. Why should they? After all, he was nobody in their eye, a mere beggar. Why should they listen to him? He then decided to go to the Parliament of Religions in Chicago. Already many people were pressing him to go there, but he was in two minds about going. Why should he, a monk, go abroad? But after the treatment he had received from the rich and the enlightened in the country, he decided he should go. He argued a knock from outside was worth ten knocks from inside. If he succeeded, in the West, people back at home would then listen to him. Our people in India were then mesmerized by the West. Later events proved how right Swamiji was. Because he had succeeded in the West, people at home gave him a hero's welcome when he returned to India.

But what exactly did Swamiji preach in the West? Did he preach Hinduism? Yes and no. Yes, to the extent that as a delegate to the Parliament of Religions, he read a remarkable paper on Hinduism and also spoke about Hinduism at different forums at the request of his hosts. No, in the sense that the main thrust of his work in the West was towards explaining the Indian identity as a whole and not any particular aspect of it. Till his appearance on the Western scene, India was a benighted country only waiting to be saved by the Christian whites. For the first time, people heard a self-respecting and knowledgeable Indian tell them that behind the facade of national poverty, India possessed a wealth of mind and spirit, accumulated over the centuries, which far out-weighed anything the West possessed in human value. For the first time, the Western audiences heard an authentic account of India's achievements in art, architecture, literarure, philosophy, even science. It was an India the West knew nothing about. It was a revelation to its people. The Western press was eloquent in its condemnation of those interested parties who had so long kept them in the dark about the glories of India. The impact that Swamiji produced in the West was very great indeed, but it was much greater in his own country. For the first time, educated Indians began to see India in her true perspective : True she was under a colonial rule resulting in abysmal poverty and backwardness, but her ancient heritage was still intact, a treasure no other country possessed. What was needed was a re-reading of her history. India's weakness was social—it lay in the neglect of the masses. She had produced a few great souls like Buddha and Sankara, but the masses had been by and large, left to themselves. They had to be educated and made conscious of their rights and privileges. He called out to the people who had received Western education and had come to believe that everything Western was good. He was not one who would say India had nothing to learn from the West. He, in fact, wanted that Indian people should learn to be efficient like the people of the West. The West had achieved much material progress which India lacked. Swamiji wanted India to apply Western technology to raise its material standards but that in doing so, she must not sacrifice her spiritual identity. India had high idealism which he wanted her to cherish by all means, but idealism was meaningless where millions starved. So coming back home, he talked more about social problems than about high philosophy. He believed that India was capable of showing the way the hopes and aspirations of the masses could be satisfied while maintaining individual and collective life at a high moral level. 'Have faith in yourselves'—this was his message. He wanted India to feel proud of herself. A nation without self-respect was dead. He would not mind assimilating new thoughts and ideas, but he would never imitate anybody. Imitation was a kind of slavery to him and he hated it.

No one in Indian history had so ably summed up India's good as well as bad points. When he praised India he would go into raptures, but when he detailed her weaknesses, he was merciless. He, however, gave back India her dignity. A nation may have problems but if it loses its self-respect, it is as good as dead.

India is indebted to Swamiji because he gave her a sense of identity. That India is a great country with a living civilization dating back to several thousand years is now an acknowledged fact. It is to Swamiji that India owes this. India re-discovered herself through him. It is to his success in the West that Indian renaissance has to be traced. Many have contributed to the making of modern India, but no one has contributed so significantly as Swami Vivekananda. What is important is that his message is still relevant. His message is modern, rational and profound. He addresses himself not to a particular community but to the whole nation, in fact to humanity itself. What he teaches is Truth, Truth which is as much applicable to an individual, as to a nation.

A

Above all and in all, be sincere. (VIII. 230)

Above all, work for the good of humanity. (III. 444)

Accept the "beneficial" and discard the "pleasant". (VII. 199)

Accord a place to everyone. (II. 351)

Accumulate power in silence and become a dynamo of spirituality. (VII. 61)

Achieve happiness or achieve greatness. (VIII. 391)

Achieve the consummation of human life before you pass off. (VI. 512)

Advance, forward, O ye brave souls, to set free those that are in fetters, to lessen the burden of woe of the miserable, and to illumine the abysmal darkness of ignorant hearts ! (VII. 504)

After having done work, do not think of it. Go on ! Stop not ! Don't look back ! What will you gain by looking back ? (II. 471)

All have to work hard ; all have to reach the depths of that infinite Energy. (VIII. 102)

All self should go out ; all superstition should be banished. (VIII. 219)

All our hatchets let us bury ; send out this grand current of love all round. (III. 380)

Always discriminate between the real and unreal, and devote yourself heart and soul to the attempt to realise the Atman. (VI. 519)

Always discriminate—your body, your house, these jivas and the world are all absolutely unreal like a dream. (VII. 194)

Always first learn to be a servant, and then you will be fit to be a master. (III. 134-35)

Always hold on to the highest. (V. 108)

Always look within, never without. (VIII. 136)

Always repeat the great Mantras—"तत्त्वमसि—Thou art that", "सोऽइमस्मि—I am that", "सर्व॰ खल्विदं ब्रह्म—All this is verily Brahman"—and have the courage of a lion in the heart. (VII. 200)

Always think that this body is only an inert instrument. And the self-contained Purusha within is your real nature. (VII. 194)

Always try to get absorbed in the eternally present Atman. (VII. 267)

A man must desire nothing else but the truth, and truth for truth's sake. (II. 407)

Analyse everything that comes in the mind by the sheer action of the will. (VI. 91)

Analyse yourselves and you will find that every blow you have received, came to you because you prepared yourselves for it. (II. 7)

And here is the test of truth—anything that makes you

weak physically, intellectually, reject as poison ; there is no life in it, it cannot be true. (III. 224-25)

Appreciation or no appreciation, sleep not, slacken not. (V. 34)

Arise and awake and be perfectly sincere. (III. 431)

Arise and awake, for the time is passing and all our energies will be frittered away in vain talking. (III. 431)

Arise and awake, let minor things, and quarrels over little details and fights over little doctrines be thrown aside, for here is the greatest of all works, here are the sinking millions. (III. 431-32)

Arise and show your manhood, your Brahminhood, by raising the non-Brahmins around you—not in the spirit of a master—not with the rotten canker of egotism crawling with superstitions and the charlatanry of East and West—but in the spirit of a servant. (IV. 300)

Arise ! Arise ! A tidal wave is coming ! Onward ! Men and women, down to the Chandala (Pariah)—all are pure in his eyes. Onward ! Onward ! There is no time to care for name, or fame, or Mukti, or Bhakti ! (VI. 294)

Arise, arise once more, for nothing can be done without renunciation. (III. 430-31)

Arise, awake ! Awake from this hypnotism of weakness. (III. 193)

"Arise, awake and stop not till the desired end is reached." (III. 320)

"Arise, awake, and stop not till the goal is reached." (III.193)

Arise, awake, for your country needs this tremendous sacrifice. (III. 318)

Arise, awake, with your hands stretched out to protect the spirituality of the world. (III. 432)

Arise, awake ; wake up yourselves, and awaken others. (VI. 512)

Arise, therefore, come forward, display the play of your superior power within, manifest it, and we are standing with offerings of deepest veneration in hand ready to worship you. (IV. 420)

Arise, Ye mighty one, and be strong ! Work on and on, struggle on and on ! (VI. 244)

As far as we can, we must give up. (IV. 180)

As you began in God, you must go back to God. (IV. 216)

Ask not anything in return for your love. (III. 88)

Ask nothing ; want nothing in return. (II. 5)

Ask, therefore, nothing in return ; but the more you give, the more will come to you. (II. 5)

Assert everything that is God. (VIII. 228)

Assert thy strength, thou Lord of lords and God of gods ! (II. 403)

As Shri Ramakrishna used to love you, as I love you, come, love the world like that. (VI. 266)

As you do good to yourself, so you must do good to others. (III. 360)

Attach yourselves to the Lord and to nothing else, because everything else is unreal. (I. 442)

Attain the supreme knowledge and go beyond Vidya and Avidya, relative knowledge and ignorance. (VII. 211)

Avoid all weakness, for weakness is sin, weakness is death. (III. 151)

Avoid all weakness if you want to be a Jnani. (III. 26)

Avoid evil company, because the scars of old wounds are in you, and evil company is just the thing that is necessary to call them out. (I. 220)

Avoid jealousy and selfishness. (V. 108)

"Avoid not and seek not—wait for what the Lord sends", is my motto. (VI. 343)

Avoid this jealousy, and you will do great works that have yet to be done. (III. 135)

Avoid weakness and slavery. (VII. 13)

Avoid worldly company, that will distract your mind. (VII.10)

Awake and arise, O mighty one, this sleep does not become you. Awake and arise, it does not befit you. Think not that you are weak and miserable. Almighty, arise and awake, and manifest your own nature. (II. 304)

Awake, arise and dream no more. (IV. 388)

Awake, arise, and stop not till the goal is reached. (II. 170)

"Awake, arise, and stop not until the goal is reached" say the Vedas. (III. 27)

Awake, awake, great ones ! The world is burning with misery. Can you sleep ? (VII. 501)

Ay, let every man and woman and child, without respect of caste or birth, weakness or strength, hear and learn that behind the strong and the weak, behind the high and the low, behind every one, there is that Infinite Soul, assuring the infinite possibility and the infinite capacity of all to become great and good. (III. 193)

B

Bar not the exit into the ocean. The moment you do that, death seizes you. (II. 5-6)

Be a hero, Always say, "I have no fear." (VII. 136)

Be a *man* and try to make those immediately under your care,...brave, moral, and sympathising. (V. 3)

Be a man first, my friend, and you will see how all those things and the rest will follow of themselves after you. (V. 462)

Be a Rishi—that is the secret of power. (III. 457)

Be always ready to concede to the opinions of your brethren, and try always to conciliate. (V. 37)

"Be and make." (IV. 351)

Be at peace. Do not disturb yourself. You never were in bondage, you never were virtuous or sinful. (VII. 74)

Be beyond both freedom and bondage. (VII. 32)

Be beyond the common worldly motives. (I. 116)

Be beyond the dualities of nature. (VI. 82)

Be bold and fear not. (III. 318)

Be bold and fearless and the road will be clear. (V. 98)

Be bold, face facts as facts. Do not be chased about the universe by evil. Evils are evils. What of that ? (VI. 149)

Be brave and be sincere ; then follow any path with devotion, and you *must* reach the Whole. (VII. 6)

Be brave and face everything—come good, come evil, both welcome, both of you my play. (VIII. 505)

Be brave, be brave ! Man dies but once. (V. 87)

Be chaste in thought, word, and action. (VI. 124)

Be content to work, and, above all, be true to yourself. (V. 57)

Be courageous. Do not try to lead your brethren, but serve them. (V. 36)

Be determined not to curse anything outside, not to lay the blame upon any one outside, but be a man, stand up, lay the blame on yourself. (II. 8)

Be earnest over this realisation and set your heart on it. (VII. 211)

Be fearless, the Lord is with you, and He will yet raise the starving and ignorant millions of India. (V. 23-24)

Be for one moment really "hopeless", and the mist will clear. For what to hope when one is the all of existence ? (VIII. 22)

Be free, and then have any number of personalities you like. Then we will play like the actor who comes upon the stage and plays the part of a beggar. (II. 323)

Be free. Death alone can never free us. (VII. 101)

Be free from the bonds of nature, be free from weakness. (III. 238)

Be free ; hope for nothing from anyone. (II. 324)

Be glad at birth, be glad at death, rejoice always in the love of God. (VIII. 18)

Be good and have mercy on those who suffer. (II. 181)

Be great. No great work can be done without sacrifice. (IV. 352)

Be grateful to the man you help, think of him as God. (I. 77)

Be holy—trust in the Lord, depend on Him always. (V. 57)

Be in no hurry therefore to give your thoughts to others. (IV. 177)

Be in the world, but not of it, like the lotus leaf whose roots are in the mud but which remains always pure. (VII. 63)

Be independent, learn to form independent judgement. (VI. 265)

Be jealous of none. (IV. 350)

Be like the pearl oyster. (I. 177)

Be masters of all these. (II. 303)

(Mother!) Be merciful and kind to me, / to chide my faults forbear. (VI. 176)

Be moral. Be brave. Be heart-whole man. Strictly moral, brave unto desperation. (V. 3)

Be not afraid. Awake, arise, and stop not till the goal is reached ! (I. 480)

Be not afraid of anything. You will do marvellous work. (III. 321)

Be not an imitation of Jesus, but be Jesus. (I. 483)

Be not compelled. Why should you be compelled ? *Everything that you do under compulsion goes to build up attachment.* (I. 104)

Be not discouraged. One word of truth can never be lost; for ages it may be hidden under rubbish, but it will show itself sooner or later. (V. 57)

Be not disheartened. When good nectar is unattainable, it is no reason why we should eat poison.(VI. 121)

Be not in despair ; the way is very difficult, like walking on the edge of a razor ; yet despair not, arise, awake, and find the ideal, the goal. (II. 124)

Be not inflated with my success or yours. Great works are to be done ; what is this small success in comparison with what is to come ? (V. 35)

"Be not of the world ; become perfectly unselfish."
(IV. 131)

Be not ruffled by vain arguments. Come to your own
realisation. You alone can do it. (VI. 88)

Be obedient and eternally faithful to the cause of truth,
humanity, and your country, and you will move the
world. (V. 108)

Be of good cheer and believe that we are selected by the
Lord to do great things, and we will do them. (V. 23)

Be one with the universe, be one with Him. (I. 381)

Be perfectly hopeless, that is the highest state. What is
there to hope for ? Burst as under the bonds of hope,
stand on your Self, be at rest, never mind what you
do, give up all to God, but have no hypocrisy about it.
(VII. 82)

Be patriots, love the race which has done such great things
for us in the past. (III. 199)

Be perfect in this idea ; and then as long as the body
endures, speak unto others this message of
fearlessness : "Thou art that", "Arise, awake, and
stop not till the goal is reached !" (VII. 213)

Be perfectly pure in money dealings. (V. 98)

Be perfectly resigned, perfectly unconcerned ; then alone
can you do any true work. (VII. 14)

Be perfectly unselfish, and you will be sure to succeed.
(V. 61)

Be positive ; do not criticise others. Give your message, teach what you have to teach, and there stop. (V. 61)

"Be possessed of *Shraddha* (faith), or *Virya* (courage), attain to the knowledge of the Atman, and sacrifice your life for the good of others—this is my wish and blessing." (VII. 267)

"Be practical". (III. 526)

Be pure and be good; be pure and love everyone. (III. 527)

Be pure, be calm ! the mind when ruffled cannot reflect the Lord. (VI. 88)

Be pure first, and you will have power. (III. 296)

Be pure. Give up superstitions and see the wonderful harmony of nature. (VIII. 218)

Be pure, staunch, and sincere to the very backbone, and everything will be all right. (V. 57)

Be ready to lend a hand to every worker of good. (IV. 350)

Be selfless. (IV. 150)

Be sincere and do your duty. (V. 54)

Be Sita. (VI. 103)

"Be spiritual and realise truth for yourself." (IV. 187)

Be steady, and, above all, be pure and sincere to the backbone. (III. 445)

Be steady. Avoid jealousy and selfishness. (V. 108)

"Be still and know that you are God." (VII. 92)

Be strong and have this *Shraddha*, and everything else is bound to follow. (III. 320)

Be strong and hopeful and unashamed, and remember that with something to take, Hindus have immeasurably more to give than any other people in the world. (V. 232)

Be strong, and stand on your own feet. (III. 279)

Be strong and stand up and seek the God of love. (IV. 60)

Be strong, get beyond all superstitions, and be free. (VIII. 187)

Be the servant if you will rule. That is the real secret. (VII. 482)

Be the servant of all. (V. 78)

Be the servant while leading. (IV. 369)

Be therefore, not a beggar, be unattached. (II. 6)

Be therefore spiritual first ; have something to give and then stand before the world and give it.(IV. 179)

Be the witness and do not react, only thus can you be happy. (VII. 49)

Be the witness. *Learn never to react*. (VIII. 230)

Be true to your mission. (V. 62)

Be true unto death. (V. 61)

Be unattached. (VII. 62)

Be "unattached"; let things work ; let brain centres work; work incessantly, but let not a ripple conquer the mind. (I. 56)

Be unselfish, and *never listen to one friend in private accusing another*. (IV. 369)

Be unselfish even unto death, and work. (V. 36)

Be you holy and, above all, sincere ; and do not for a moment give up your trust in the Lord, and you will see the light. (VIII. 381)

Be you my helpers in this work ! Go from village to village, from one portion of the country to another, and preach this message of fearlessness to all, from the Brahmin to the Chandala. (VII. 182)

Be your own Self. (V. 275)

Bear all evil and misery without one murmur of hurt, without one thought of unhappiness, resistance, remedy, or retaliation. (VIII. 110)

Bear in mind, my children, that only cowards and those who are weak commit sin and tell lies. (V. 3)

Bear with the various opinions of everybody. Patience, purity, and perseverance will prevail. (V. 62)

Become perfectly unselfish, ready to give up your life even for an ant. (VIII. 99)

Become Radha and be saved. (VI. 116)

Before flooding India with socialistic or political ideas, first deluge the land with spiritual ideas. (III. 221)

Beget no evil. (VI. 124)

Begin with disbelief. Analyse, test, prove everything, and then take it. (II. 28)

Believe first in yourself, then in God. (VIII. 223)

Believe in India and in our Indian faith. (V. 232)

Believe in man first. Why start with the belief that man is degraded and degenerated ? (III. 383)

Believe nothing until you find it out for yourself. (I. 131-32)

Believe in nothing until you *know* it. (VIII. 4)

Believe in that infinite soul, the infinite power, which, with consensus of opinion, your books and sages preach. (III. 319)

Believe not that we are evil, that we are finite, that we can ever die. (II. 405)

Believe that the soul is immortal, infinite and all-powerful (V. 224)

Believe, therefore, in yourselves. The secret of Advaita is: Believe in yourselves first, and then believe in anything else. (III. 426)

Better die than live that life. Slaves of this world, slaves of the senses, let us rouse ourselves ; there is something higher than this sense-life. (IV. 17)

Beware of everything that takes away your freedom. (I. 173)

Beware of falsehood. (V. 37)

Blame neither man, nor God, nor anyone in the world. When you find yourselves suffering, blame yourselves, and try to do better. (II. 225)

Blame none ; if evil comes, know the Lord is playing with you and be exceeding glad. (VII. 11)

Blame none for your own faults, stand upon your own feet, and take the whole responsibility upon yourselves. (II. 225)

Bless men when they revile you. Think how much good they are doing by helping to stamp out the false ego. (VIII. 31)

Bow down to nothing but your own higher Self. (VII. 78)

Break that chain and be free. (II. 323)

Break your chain and be free for ever. What frightens you, what holds you down ? Only ignorance and delusion; nothing else can bind you. (II. 236-37)

Bring about the golden days when every man will be a worshipper, and the Reality in every man will be the object of worship. (II. 358)

Bring all light into the world. (III. 247)

Bring all the forces of good together. Do not care under what banner you march. Do not care what be your colour—green, blue, or red—but mix up all the colours and produce that intense glow of white, the colour of love. (IV. 352-53)

Bring forth the power of the spirit, and pour it over the length and breadth of India ; and all that is necessary will come by itself. (IV. 351)

Bring in the light ; the darkness will vanish of itself. (IV. 351)

Bring in the light and the evil goes in a moment. (II. 357)

Bring light to all and leave the rest unto the Lord. (III. 247)

Bring light to the ignorant, and more light to the educated, for the vanities of the education of our time are tremendous ! (III. 247)

Bring light to the poor ; and bring more light to the rich, for they require it more than the poor. (III. 247)

Bring out through your own exertions what you have, but do not imitate, yet take what is good from others. (III. 381)

Bring truth out ! (VIII. 96)

Bring your own lotus to blossom; the bees will come of themselves. (VIII. 223)

Build up your character, and manifest your real nature, the Effulgent, the Resplendent, the Ever-Pure, and call It up in everyone that you see. (II. 357)

Build your hope on none. (V. 34)

"Burn virtue, burn vice." (VII. 73)

Burst asunder the bonds of hope, stand on your Self, be at rest, never mind what you do, give up all to God, but have no hypocrisy about it. (VII. 82)

But bold we must be. Hiding facts is not the way to find a remedy. (II. 94)

C

Call up the divinity within you, which will enable you to bear hunger and thirst, heat and cold. (IV. 352)

Cast off all fear—though these horrible ideas of God as a punisher or rewarder may have their use in savage minds. (II. 49)

Cast into the fire/all thy dross of self, thy mean selfishness.
(IV. 496)

Cease not to say day and night—THY WILL BE DONE.
(IV. 355)

Choose the highest ideal, and give your life up to that.
(VII. 45)

Cleanse the mind, this is all of religion ; and until we
ourselves clear off the spots, we cannot see the
Reality as it is. (VII. 75)

Cleanse the spirit, and it (the kingdom of God) is there.
(IV. 149)

Combine seriousness with childlike *naïveté*. (VI. 329)

Come ! Apply yourselves heart and soul to it. The day of
gossip and ceremonials is gone, my boy, *you must
work now*. (VI. 290)

Come, be men ! Come out of your narrow holes and have
a look abroad. (V. 10)

Come on to the practical field with tremendous energy ; to
work, in the fullness of strength ! (VI. 278)

Come out if you can of this network of foolishness they
call this *world*. Then I will call you indeed brave and
free. (V. 72)

Come out into the universe of Light. Everything in the
universe is yours, stretch out your arms and embrace
it with love. (II. 323)

Come public women, come drunkards, come thieves and
all—His gate is open to all. (VI. 370)

Come what will, we must give our bodies and minds up to
the Supreme Will. (I. 343)

Come ye that are heavy laden and lay all your burden on
me, and then do whatever you like and be happy and
forget that I ever existed. (VII. 521)

Condemn none ; if you can stretch out a helping hand, do
so. (II. 299)

Conquer *yourself*, and the whole universe is yours.
(VII. 15)

Consciousness, therefore, is the chief thing to be
understood. (II. 33)

Continue to exercise your will and it will take you higher
still. (II. 356)

Control the senses. (VIII. 228)

Cultivate always "faith in yourself". (V. 52)

Cultivate the virtue of obedience, but you must not
sacrifice your own faith. (V. 78)

Cut off all desire. (VII. 66)

Cut the bondage of all worldly affections ; go beyond
laziness and all care as to what becomes of you.
(VII. 10)

D

Dare to be free, dare to go as far as your thought leads,
and dare to carry that out in your life. (III. 11)

Dare to seek Truth even through hell. (VIII. 32)

Day and night say, "I am He". It is the greatest strength ;
it is religion. (III. 26)

Day and night tell yourself, "I am He, I am He."
(VIII. 6)

Death has caught you by the forelock...still fear not.
(VIII. 432)

Deepen your own power of thought and love.
(VIII. 223)

Deny evil, create none. (VII. 54)

Desire nothing except God. This world is good so far as it
helps one to go to the higher world. (IV. 7)

Desire nothing for yourself. Do all for others. This is to live
and move and have your being in God.
(VI. 83)

"Desire nothing, give up all desires and be perfectly
satisfied." (II. 261)

Desire nothing ; think of God and look for no return. It is
the desireless who bring results. (VII. 14)

Determine your own nature and stick to it. *Nishtha*
(devotion to one ideal) is the only method for the
beginner ; but with devotion and sincerity it will lead
to all. (VII. 6)

Die if you must. There is none to help you. You are all the
world. Who can help you ? (I. 461)

Die in obeying commands like a soldier, and go to Nirvana,
but no cowardice. (VIII. 482)

Discard fear (*mabhaih, mabhaih*). Let not your faith be
shaken. ... Has danger any power over one whom
the Lord has taken into His fold ? (VI. 342)

Dis-identify yourself with the body, and all pain will cease. This is the secret of healing. (VII. 46)

Do all without regard to personal result, give up all results to the Lord, then neither good nor evil will affect you. (VII. 69)

Do everything but do not get identified with anything. (IV. 96)

"Do good and be good. And this will take you to freedom and to whatever truth there is." (I. 117)

Do good to all, like everyone, but *do not love* anyone. (VIII. 414)

Do not be afraid. (V. 110)

Do not be cowardly and hypocritical. (VI. 121)

Do not be dragged away out of this Indian life ; do not for a moment think that it would be better for India if all the Indians dressed, ate, and behaved like another race. (III. 382)

Do not be frightened. Awake, be up and doing. Do not stop till you have reached the goal. (II. 410)

Do not be in a hurry, do not go out to imitate anybody else. (III. 381)

Do not believe in anything unquestioningly. (IV. 216)

Do not believe that you are weak. (III. 284)

Do not be jealous of anyone. Look not to the faults of others. (V. 410)

Do not be miserable ! do not repent ! What is done is done. (II. 471)

Do not be proud ; Do not insist upon anything dogmatic ; do not go against anything—ours is to put chemicals together, the Lord knows how and when the crystal will form. (V. 35)

Do not care for anybody to help you. Is not the Lord infinitely greater than all human help ? (V. 57)

Do not care what be your lot. (V. 253)

Do not choose dirty places. Rather choose beautiful scenery, or a room in your own house which is beautiful. (I. 192)

Do not decry these rituals and mythologies. Let people have them; let those who so desire have them. (II. 393)

Do not delay a moment. Leave nothing for tomorrow. Get ready for the final event, which may overtake you immediately, even now. (IV. 132-33)

Do not desire anything. What makes us miserable ? The cause of all miseries from which we suffer is desire. (II.147)

Do not desire, for what you desire you get, and with it comes terrible bondage. (VII. 90)

Do not despair ! (I. 521)

Do not despair, and do not drag the ideal down. (VIII. 120)

Do not destroy. Iconoclastic reformers do no good to the world. Break not, pull not anything down, but build. Help, if you can ; if you cannot, fold your hands and

stand by and see things go on. Do not injure, if you
cannot render help. Say not a word against any
man's convictions so far as they are sincere.
(II. 384)

Do not disturb, but help everyone to get higher and
higher; include all humanity. (II. 141)

Do not disturb the faith of any. For you must know that
religion is not in doctrines. (VIII. 229)

Do not disturb your mind by vain arguments. (II. 408)

Do not drag others down to where you are. (II. 351)

Do not exercise too hard; it is injurious. (VI. 101)

Do not fight with people; do not antagonise anyone.
(V. 62)

Do not fight over methods. Look only for realisation and
choose the best method you can find to suit you.
(VII. 65)

Do not fly away from the wheels of the world-machine,
but stand inside it and learn the secret of work.
(I. 115)

Do not for a moment quail. Everything will come all right.
It is will that moves the world. (V. 47)

Do not forget the great ideal of our religion, that great ideal
of the Hindus. (III. 453)

Do not give up anything in nature. Make it so hot for
nature that she will give you up. (I. 519)

Do not give up anything ! Things will give you up.
(VI. 73)

Do not give up the world ; live in the world, imbibe its
 influences as much as you can ; but if it be for your
 own enjoyment's sake, work not at all. (I. 88)

Do not go about throwing mud at others ; for all the faults
 you suffer from, you are the sole and only cause.
 (III. 429)

Do not go for glass beads leaving the mine of diamonds !
 This life is a great chance. (VI. 262)

Do not hate anybody, because that hatred which comes
 out from you, must, in the long run, come back to
 you. (I. 196)

Do not identify yourself with anything. Hold your mind
 free. All this that you see, the pains and miseries, are
 but the necessary conditions of this world ; poverty
 and wealth and happiness are but momentary ; they
 do not belong to our real nature at all. (I. 100)

Do not injure another. Love everyone as your own self,
 because the whole universe is One. In injuring
 another, I am injuring myself ; in loving another, I am
 loving myself. (I. 364)

Do not injure any being ; not injuring any being is virtue,
 injuring any being is sin. (I. 64)

Do not lay the blame upon anybody. (I. 497)

Do not let nature raise the wave. Keep quiet, and then
 after a little while she will give you up . (IV. 248)

Do not let the thoughts grasp you ; stand aside, and they
 will die away. (VIII. 50)

Do not let these weaknesses and failures bind you. (I. 342)

Do not limit God anywhere. (IV. 31)

Do not look to others for help. (V. 65)

Do not look upon humanity as the centre of all your human and higher interests. (III. 74)

Do not lose heart, do not lose faith in your Guru, do not lose faith in God. (V. 74)

Do not make the lamp burn fast ; let it burn slowly. (VI. 102)

Do not merely endure, be unattached. (VII. 14)

Do not pity anyone. Look upon all as your equal, cleanse yourself of the primal sin of inequality. (VIII. 18)

Do not practise (Yoga) when the body feels very lazy or ill, or when the mind is very miserable and sorrowful. (I. 192)

Do not pray for little things. If you seek only bodily comforts, where is the difference between men and animals ? (IV. 38)

Do not recognise wickedness in others. (VI. 141)

Do not run after the manifold ; go towards the One. (II.182)

Do not run after these superstitions. (III. 279)

Do not run away, it is cowardice. When in the thing, you must do it. (VI. 113)

Do not say we are weak ; we can do anything and everything. What can we not do ? Everything can be done by us ; we all have the same glorious soul, let us believe in it. (III. 244)

Do not seek help from anyone. We are our own help. (I. 478)

Do not sit idle, thinking that everything will be done in time, later on ! Mind—nothing will be done that way ! (V. 384)

Do not spend your energy in talking, but meditate in silence ; and do not let the rush of the outside world disturb you. (VII. 61)

Do not take any hasty step. (VI. 280-81)

Do not talk much, but feel the spirit within you. (VII. 81)

Do not talk of God when you see matter. (III. 421)

Do not talk religion. (II. 474)

Do not tarry—the time of death is approaching day by day. (V. 384)

Do not try by contrivances to control the mind ; simple breathing is all that is necessary in that line. (VI. 39)

Do not try to be a ruler. He is the best ruler who can serve well. (V. 61)

Do not try to "boss" others. (IV. 369)

Do not try to disturb the faith of any man. If you can, give him something better ; if you can, get hold of a man where he stands and give him a push upwards. (IV. 183)

Do not try to fly. (VI. 83)

Do not wait for anybody or anything. (V. 34)

Do not want this world. (VII. 63)

Do not weaken ! There is no other way out. ...Stand up and be strong ! No fear. (I. 479)

Don't allow egoism to enter your minds, and let love never depart from your hearts. (VIII. 481)

Don't bother your head with religious theories. (V. 3)

Don't despond in the least. (VIII. 522)

Don't enter into wrangles with anybody—always maintain a calm attitude. (VIII. 397)

Don't look back—forward, infinite energy, infinite enthusiasm, infinite daring, and infinite patience— then alone can great deeds be accomplished. (VIII. 353)

Don't nod assent like a fool to everything said. Don't put implicit faith, even if I declare something. First clearly grasp and then accept. (VI. 501)

Don't worry in the least ; heaven or hell, or Bhakti or Mukti—don't care for anything, but go, my boy, and spread the name of the Lord from door to door. (VI. 266)

Do one thing at a time and while doing it put your whole soul into it to the exclusion of all else. (VI. 89)

"Do rely on Him ; be like the dry leaf at the mercy of the wind." (VI. 481)

Do something ! Do something ! (VI. 65)

Do something for the nation, then they will help you, then the nation will be with you. (V. 87)

Do something for your souls ! Do wrong if you please, but do something ! (VI. 66)

Do something. Think some thought ; it doesn't matter whether you are right or wrong. (IV. 127)

Do things for others ; Expand ! (II. 466)

Do this either by work, or worship, or psychic control, or philosophy—by one or more or all of these—and be free. (I. 257)

Down with all sloth, down with all enjoyments here or hereafter. (V. 66)

Draw near the centre, check desire, stamp it out, let the false self go, then our vision will clear and we shall see God. (VIII. 22)

Dream no more ! (V. 72)

Drink deep of the nectar of the knowledge of God. (VI. 82)

E

Each must follow his own religion. (VIII. 315)

Each must verify for himself. (VII. 9)

Each one must have his own way. (V. 301)

Each one of us will have to discover. (VI. 14)

Electrify people. (V. 62)

Enter not the door of any organised religion. (I. 474)

Enter ye into the realms of light, the gates have been opened wide once more. (IV. 329)

Enveloped in *Tamas* however much you may be, know all

that will clear away if you take refuge in Him by being sincere to the core of your heart. (V. 358)

Even if the order be wrong, first obey and then contradict it. (III. 448)

Even if you are at your last breath, be not afraid. (VI. 332)

Even these earthworms must stand erect, even children must see light. (V. 137)

Ever tell yourself, "I am He." These are words that will burn up the dross that is in the mind, words that will bring out the tremendous energy which is within you already, the infinite power which is sleeping in your heart. (III. 26)

Every idea that strengthens you must be taken up and every thought that weakens you must be rejected. (III. 27)

Every man must develop according to his own nature. (V. 292)

Every work should be made thorough. (V. 75)

Everyone should learn to obey before he can command. (V. 216)

Expect nothing in return. (I. 59)

F

Face the terrible, face it boldly. (I. 338)

Face the truth as it is ! (I. 480)

Faith, sympathy-fiery faith and fiery sympathy. (V. 17)

Fear nothing. (I. 47)

Feed the national life with the fuel it wants, but the growth
is its own ; none can dictate its growth to it.
(III. 213)

Feel first for the world. (VI. 145)

Feel for the miserable and look up for help—it *shall come.*
(V. 16)

Feel, my children, feel ; feel for the poor, the ignorant, the
downtrodden ; feel till the heart stops and the brain
reels and you think you will go mad—then pour the
soul out at the feet of the Lord, and then will come
the power, help, and indomitable energy.
(IV. 367)

Feel nothing, know nothing, do nothing, have nothing, give
up all to God, and say utterly, "Thy will be done".
(VII. 68)

Feel that you are great and you become great.
(III. 243)

Fight and reason and argue ; and when you have
established it in your mind that this alone can be the
truth and nothing else, do not argue any more ; close
your mouth. (III. 27)

Fight it out, whatever comes. Let the stars move from the
sphere ! Let the whole world stand against us !
Death means only a change of garment. (I. 461)

Fight on bravely ! Life is short ! Give it up to a great cause.
(V. 37)

Fill the brain, therefore, with high thoughts, highest ideals, place them day and night before you, and out of that will come great work. Talk not about impurity, but say that we are pure. (II. 86)

Fill the mind (with it) day and night : "I am it. I am the Lord of the universe. Never was there any delusion." (I. 501)

Fill the mind with the highest thoughts, hear them day after day, think them month after month. (II. 152)

Fill yourselves with the ideal ; whatever you do, think well on it. (II. 302)

"Find it out, thou art That." (I. 141)

Find out the truth about God and about your own soul and thus attain to liberation. (IV. 232)

First be master of yourself, stand up and be free, go beyond the pale of these laws, for these laws do not absolutely govern you, they are only part of your being. (II. 181-82)

First deluge the land (India) with spiritual ideas, then other ideas will follow. (V. 267)

First feel from the heart. What is in the intellect or reason? It goes a few steps and there it stops. (III. 225)

First form character, first earn spirituality and results will come of themselves. (IV. 177)

First get rid of the delusion, "I am the body", then only can we want real knowledge. (VII. 33)

First, have faith in yourselves. Know that though one may be a little bubble and another may be a mountain-high wave, yet behind both the bubble and the wave there is the infinite ocean. (III. 444)

First have something to give. (IV. 177)

First, learn to obey. (III. 134)

First, let us be Gods, and then help others to be Gods. (IV. 351)

First make character—that is the highest duty you can perform. (IV. 178)

First make yourselves pure. (III. 258)

First of all, our young men must be strong. Religion will come afterwards. Be strong, my young friends ; that is my advice to you. (III. 242)

First purify yourself by work and devotion. (VI. 281)

First root out this idea of helping, and then go to worship. (I. 442)

First rouse the inherent power of the Atman within you, then, rousing the faith of the general people in that power as much as you can, teach them first of all to make provision for food, and then teach them religion. (VII. 183)

First there should be strict integrity.... Secondly, entire devotion to the cause.... (V. 111)

Follow God and you shall have whatever you desire. (V. 245)

Follow the heart. A pure heart sees beyond the intellect ; it
gets inspired ; it knows things that reason can never
know, and whenever there is conflict between the
pure heart and the intellect, always side with the
pure heart even if you think what your heart is doing
is unreasonable. (I. 414)

Follow truth wherever it may lead you ; carry ideas to their
utmost logical conclusions. (VI. 121)

Forget first the love for gold and name and fame, and for
this little trumpery world of ours. (III. 259)

Forget not that the ideal of thy womanhood is Sita, Savitri,
Damayanti ; forget not that the God thou
worshippest is the great Ascetic of ascetics, the all-
renouncing Shankara, the Lord of Uma ; forget not
that thy marriage, thy wealth, thy life are not for
sense-pleasure, are not for thy individual personal
happiness ; forget not that thou art born as a
sacrifice to the Mother's altar ; forget not that thy
social order is but the reflex of the Infinite Universal
Motherhood ; forget not that the lower classes, the
ignorant, the poor, the illiterate, the cobbler, the
sweeper, are thy flesh and blood, thy brothers.
(IV. 479-80)

Forget yourselves ; this is the first lesson to be learnt.
Whether you are theist or an atheist, whether you
are an agnostic or Vedantist, a Christian or a
Mohammedan. (II. 353)

G

Gain independence, gain everything, but do not lose that characteristic of woman ! (I. 481)

Get away from all books and forms and let your soul see its Self. (VI. 82)

Get hold of any one of these chains (ceremonies, books and forms) that are stretched out from the common centre. (I. 439)

Get hold of the mind. The mind is like a lake, and every stone that drops into it raises waves. (IV. 248)

Get rid of all other thoughts. Everything else must be thrown aside, and this is to be repeated continually, poured through the ears until it reaches the heart, until every nerve and muscle, every drop of blood tingles with the idea that I am He, I am He. (III. 25-26)

Get rid of the little "I", and let only the great "I" live. (VII. 14)

Get rid of this puny "I"; kill this diabolism in us ; "Not I, but Thou"—say it, feel it, live it. (VII. 15)

Get up, and put your shoulders to the wheel. (V. 383)

Gird up your loins. (V. 15)

Give all to the Lord and go on and think not of it. (VII. 10)

"Give", "Give away". (IV. 496)

Give me a genuine man ; I do not want masses of converts. (V. 57)

Give me a straightforward man or woman. (IV. 58)

Give the last bit of bread you have even if you are starving. (IV. 10-11)

Give this life for the service of others. (VII. 247)

Give to the weak, for there all the gift is needed. (III. 193)

Give up all argumentation and other distractions. Is there anything in dry intellectual jargon ? It only throws the mind off its balance and disturbs it. (I. 176)

"Give up all desire and be at peace. Have neither friends nor foes, and live alone. Thus shall we travel having neither friends nor foes, neither pleasure nor pain, neither desire nor jealousy, injuring no creatures, being the cause of injury to no creature—from mountain to mountain, from village to village, preaching the name of the Lord." (VI. 300)

Give up all desire for enjoyment in earth or heaven. (VII. 92)

Give up all evil company, especially at the beginning. (VII.10)

Give up all "me and mine". (VII. 10)

Give up all self, all egotism ; get out of anger, lust, *give all* to God. (VII. 11)

Give up all vain talk. Read only those books which have been written by persons who have had realisation. (I.176-77)

Give up being a slave. (III. 300)

Give up bondage ; become a son, be free, and then you can "see the Father", as did Jesus. (VII. 13)

Give up desire. (VII. 91)

Give up everything for the sake of the Lord. This is hard and long task, but you can begin it here and now. But by bit we must go towards it. (IV. 180)

Give up for ever the desire for name and fame and power. (VI. 330)

Give up hope, says the Vedanta. Why should you hope ? You *have* everything, nay, you are everything. (II. 324)

Give up lust and gold and fame and hold fast to the Lord, and at last we shall reach a state of perfect indifference. (VII. 15-16)

Give up, renounce the world. Now we are like dogs strayed into a kitchen and eating a piece of meat, looking round in fear lest at any moment someone may come and drive them out. ...This never comes until you give it up and it ceases to bind. Give up (the world) mentally, if you do not physically. Give up (the world) from the heart of your hearts. (VII. 90)

"Give up," says the Veda, "give up." (III. 343)

Give up the burden of all deeds to the Lord ; give all, both good and bad. (VII. 91)

Give up the delusion, and the whole thing vanishes. (II. 198)

Give up the fruits unto Him. Let us stand aside and think
that we are only servants obeying the Lord, our
Master, and that every impulse for action comes
from Him every moment. (I. 102)

Give up the small for the Infinite, give up small enjoyments
for infinite bliss. (II. 323)

Give up the so-called boast of your narrow orthodox life.
(III. 444)

Give up the world—this nonsense of the senses. There is
only one real desire : to know what is true, to be
spiritual. (VIII. 118)

Give up the world which you have conjectured, because
your conjecture was based upon a very partial
experience, upon very poor reasoning, and upon your
own weakness. (II.146)

Give up these weakening mysticisms and be strong.
(III. 225)

Give up this little life of yours. What matters it if you die of
starvation—you and I and thousands like us—so
long as this nation lives ? (III. 431)

"Give up what is evil and give up what is good."
(II. 181)

Give up your passive attitude, gird up your loins, and stand
up. (VI. 293)

Go and preach to all, "Arise, awake, sleep no more ;
within each of you there is the power to remove all
wants and all miseries. Believe this, and that power
will be manifested." (VI. 454)

Go and tell all, "In every one of you lies that Eternal Power", and try to wake It up. (V. 383)

Go back, go back to the old days when there was strength and vitality. Be strong once more, drink deep of this fountain of yore and that is the only condition of life in India. (III. 347)

Go back to your Upanishads—the shining, strengthening, the bright philosophy—and part from all these mysterious things, all these weakening things. (III. 225)

Go beyond law, let the whole universe vanish, and stand alone. (III. 18)

Go forth into the Eternal and come back with eternal energy. The slave goes out to search for truth ; he comes back free. (VI. 83)

Go forward, and do not pay too much attention to the nature of the work you have to do. (IV. 131)

Go forward : assert yourself again and again, and light must come. (II. 403)

Go from village to village, do good to humanity and to the world at large. Go to hell yourself to buy salvation for others. (VI. 265-66)

Go on bravely. Do not expect success in a day or a year. (V. 108)

Go on doing good, thinking holy thoughts continuously ; that is the only way to suppress base impressions. (I. 208)

Go on loving. If a man is angry, there is no reason why you should be angry ; if he degrades himself, that is no reason why you should degrade yourself. (VI. 75)

Go on ; remember—patience and purity and courage and steady work. (V. 96)

Go on saying, "I am free". (I. 501)

Go on spreading love, love that knows no bounds. (VI. 267)

Go on working. (VI. 455)

Go on, work, only mind that you are not attached. (I. 465)

"Go on working without an eye to the result. One day you are sure to reap the fruits of it." (VII. 237)

Go the other way, think of God ; let the mind not think of any physical or mental enjoyment, but of God alone. (IV. 8)

Go to God directly. No theories, no doctrines. Then alone will all doubts vanish. Then alone will all crookedness be made straight. (II. 474)

H

Hate not the most abject sinner, look not to his exterior. (IV. 110)

Have charity towards all beings. Pity those who are in distress. Love all creatures. Do not be jealous of anyone. Look not to the faults of others. (V. 410)

Have faith. (V. 13)

Have faith, as Nachiketa. (III. 244)

Have faith in man, whether he appears to be an angel or the very devil himself. (III. 383-84)

Have faith in the Lord. (V. 16)

Have faith in your destiny. (III. 445)

Have faith in yourself—all power is in you—be conscious and bring it out. (VI. 274)

Have faith in yourselves, and stand up on that faith and be strong ; that is what we need. (III. 190)

Have faith in yourselves, great convictions are the mothers of great deeds. (V. 30)

Have faith ! Onward ! Great Lord ! (VI. 295)

Have infinite patience, and success is yours. (IV. 369)

Have mercy on others. (III. 424)

Have no idea of proprietorship, possessorship. (II. 148)

Have patience and be faithful unto death. (V. 98)

Have patience and work. (V. 48)

Have patience, perseverance, and purity. (V. 61)

Have that faith, each one of you, in yourself—that eternal power is lodged in every soul— and you will revive the whole of India. (II. 303)

Have thou no home. (IV. 395)

He who wants to serve the father must serve the children first. He who wants to serve Shiva must serve His children—must serve all creatures in this world first. (III. 142)

Hear day and night that you are that Soul. Repeat it to yourselves day and night till it enters into your very veins, till it tingles in every drop of blood, till it is in your flesh and bone. (II. 302)

Help and not fight. (I. 24)

Help another because you are in him and he is in you. (V. 285)

Help, if you can ; but do not destroy. (II. 385)

Help thyself out by thyself. None else can help thee, friend. For thou alone art thy greatest enemy, thou alone art thy greatest friend. (II. 403)

His will be done. (V. 23)

Hold fast to the real Self, think only pure thoughts, and you will accomplish more than a regiment of mere preachers. Out of purity and silence comes the word of power. (VIII. 31-32)

Hold fast to your only true aim—God. (VIII. 51)

Hold on to one of these links, (ceremonies, books, and forms) and it will pull you to the centre. (I. 439)

Hold on to the ideal. March on ! Do not look back upon little mistakes and things. In this battlefield of ours, the dust of mistakes must be raised. Those who are so thin-skinned that they cannot bear the dust, let them get out of the ranks. (V. 253)

Hold on with faith and strength ; be true, be honest, be pure, and don't quarrel among yourselves. Jealousy is the bane of our race. (V. 99)

Hold your life a sacrifice for the welfare of others ; and if you choose the life of renunciation, do not even look at beauty and money and power. (I. 51)

Hold yourself as a witness and go on working. (I. 88)

Hold yourself in readiness, i.e. be pure and holy, and love for love's sake. (V. 23)

Hope and do not despair. (V. 47)

I

Identify yourself only with God. (VIII. 50)

If I am in the dark, let me light a lamp. (VIII. 131)

If there is a God we must see Him, if there is a soul we must perceive it ; otherwise it is better not to believe. (I. 127)

If we really want to be blessed, and make others blessed, we must go deeper. The first step is not to disturb the mind, not to associate with persons whose ideas are disturbing. (I. 177)

If you have, then give. (IV. 124)

If you want any good to come, just throw your ceremonials overboard and worship the Living God, the Man-God–every being that wears a human form—God in His universal as well as individual aspect. (VI. 264)

If you want to be spiritual, you must renounce. (VIII. 118)

In a conflict between the heart and the brain follow your heart. (VIII. 223)

In His name and with eternal faith in Him, set fire to the mountain of misery that has been heaped upon India for ages—and it shall be burned down. (V. 17)

In religion, as in all other matters, discard everything that weakens you, have nothing to do with it. (I. 134)

In this world of Maya one need not injure, but "spread the hood, without striking". That is enough. (VIII. 495)

Injure no living creature. (VI. 124)

Injure none, deny the position of none ; take man where he stands and, if you can, lend him a helping hand and put him on a higher platform, but do not injure and do not destroy. All will come to truth in the long run. (II. 253)

It is selfishness that we must seek to eliminate. (VIII. 265)

It won't do to become impatient—wait, wait—patience is bound to give success. (VI. 284)

J

Jealousy is the bane of all slaves. It is the bane of our nation. Avoid that always. (V. 108)

Just play with the Lord. Say, "It is all play, it is all play." (VIII. 262)

K

Keep on steadily. (V. 38)

Keep the ideal in view and work towards it. (V. 125)

Keep the motto before you—"Elevation of the masses without injuring their religion." (V. 29)

Keep the spirit of discrimination along with Bhakti. (V. 347)

Keep to the ideal. (IV. 145)

'Keep yourself holy, and pure.' (II. 507)

Kill out this differentiation, kill out this superstition that there are many. (II. 252)

Kill self first if you want to succeed. (V. 83)

Know it for certain that you are in everything. (II. 472)

Know, my soul, / You are Divine. (VIII. 163)

Know once for all that I am He. (VIII. 164)

Know that talking ill of others in private is a sin. (VI. 304)

Know that the Lord is with us, and so, onward, brave soul! (V. 34)

Know that the mind which is born to succeed joins itself to a determined will and perseveres. (VI. 83)

Know that there is no darkness around us. Take the hands away and there is the light which was from the beginning. Darkness never existed, weakness never existed. (II. 295)

Know that this world is not we, nor are we this world. (I. 116)

Know that you are always free. (II. 471)

"Know the Atman alone and give up all other vain
    words." (VIII. 385)

Know this and be free. (II. 462)

Know Truth for yourself. (IV. 178)

Know you are the Infinite, then fear must die. Say ever, "I
    and my Father are one." (VII. 7)

L

Lay down your comforts, your pleasures, your names,
    fame or position, nay even your lives, and make a
    bridge of human chains over which millions will
    cross this ocean of life. (IV. 352)

Learn everything that is good from others, but bring it in,
    and in your own way absorb it ; do not become
    others. (III. 382)

"Learn good knowledge with all devotion from the lowest
    caste." (III. 151)

Learn obedience first. (VI. 349)

Learn that the whole of life is giving, that nature will force
    you to give. (II. 5)

Learn to see things in the proper light. (I. 441)

Learn to work unitedly for others. (V. 79)

Leave inimical thoughts aside if you want to have
    permanent Bhakti. (III. 358)

Leave the fruits alone. (I. 33)

Let all our actions—eating, drinking, and everything that we do—tend towards the sacrifice of our self. (III. 446)

Let all your nerves vibrate through the backbone of your religion. (III. 220)

Let an endless stream of love go forth. Let us all be men. (II. 517)

Let darkness go. (IV. 393)

Let each one of us pray day and night for the downtrodden millions in India who are held fast by poverty, priestcraft, and tyranny—pray day and night for them. (V. 58)

Let each one work out one's own salvation. (V. 147)

Let every one be taught that the divine is within, and every one will work out his own salvation. (III. 246)

Let every one do the best he can for realising his own ideal. (I. 41)

Let everyone do what little he can. (III. 245)

Let everyone go on doing his own duty unconcerned. (V. 330)

Let everything go but that One Existence. (III. 25)

Let him who has courage in his mind and love in his heart come with me. (VI. 315)

Let him work, let him fight, let him strike straight from the shoulder. (I. 39)

Let men have light, let them be pure and spiritually strong
and educated, then alone will misery cease in the
world, not before. (I. 53)

Let men have the light of liberty. That is the only condition
of growth. (II. 115)

Let name and fame and money go ; they are a terrible
bondage. (VII. 61)

Let never more delusive dreams veil off Thy face from
me. (VI. 177)

Let not the fire die out. (III. 205)

Let not your hold of that banner (renunciation) go. Hold it
aloft. Even if you are weak and cannot renounce, do
not lower the ideal. (III. 344)

Let nothing stand between God and your love for
Him.(VII. 9)

Let positive, strong, helpful thought enter into their brains
from very childhood. (II. 87)

Let that faith be spread over the whole land. (III. 445)

"Let the end and the means be joined into one." (I. 71)

Let the fruits take care of themselves. (IV. 159)

Let the grand symphony go on. (II. 483)

Let the heart be opened first, and all else will follow of
itself. (V. 346)

Let the lion of Vedanta roar ; the foxes will fly to their
holes. (IV. 351)

Let them all know what they are, let them repeat day and
night what they are. *Soham*. (III. 426)

Let them not give up their God, let them not forget that they are the children of the sages. (IV. 160)

Let them suck it in with their mother's milk, this idea of strength—I am He, I am He. (III. 426)

Let there be a dozen such lion-souls in each country, lions who have broken their own bonds, who have touched the Infinite, whose whole soul is gone to Brahman, who care neither for wealth nor power nor fame, and these will be enough to shake the world. (VIII. 348)

Let there be action without reaction. (VII. 49)

Let there be as little materialism as possible, with the maximum of spirituality. (VI. 333)

Let these people be your God—think of them, work for them, pray for them incessantly—the Lord will show you the way. (V. 58)

Let things come as they may. (III. 84)

Let us all help the onward march of accumulated goodness, for goodness' sake. (VII. 429)

Let us ask ourselves each day, "Do we want God." When we begin to talk high religion, and especially when we take a high position and begin to teach others, we must ask ourselves the same question. (IV. 20)

Let us be as progressive as any nation that ever existed, and at the same time as faithful and conservative towards our traditions as Hindus alone know how to be. (III. 174)

Let us be at peace, perfect peace, with ourselves, and give up our whole body and mind and everything as an eternal sacrifice unto the Lord. (I. 102)

Let us be brave. Know the Truth and practise the Truth. The goal may be distant, but awake, arise, and stop not till the goal is reached. (II. 87)

Let us blame none, let us blame our own Karma. (III. 166)

Let us do good because it is good to do good ; he who does good work even in order to get to heaven binds himself down. (I. 116)

Let us do that duty which is ours by birth ; and when we have done that, let us do the duty which is ours by our position in life and in society. (I. 66)

Let us get rid of the little "I " and let only the great "I" live in us. (VIII. 31)

Let us go forward and do yet greater things. (III. 196)

"Let us help, and not destroy." (VII. 422)

Let us help one another, let us love one another. (V. 413)

Let us live in Him and stand in Him. It is the only joyful state of existence. (II. 174)

Let us not be in a hurry ; everything will come by the grace of the Lord. (V. 31)

Let us not depend upon the world for pleasure. (VIII. 29)

Let us open ourselves to the one Divine Actor, and let Him act, and do nothing ourselves. (VII. 14)

Let us perfect the means ; the end will take care of itself. For the world can be good and pure, only if our lives are good and pure. It is an effect, and we are the means. Therefore, let us purify ourselves. Let us make ourselves perfect. (II. 9)

Let us pray, "Lead, Kindly Light"—a beam will come through the dark, and a hand will be stretched forth to lead us. (V. 57-58)

Let us put forth all our energies to acquire that which never fails—our spiritual perfection. (II. 37)

Let us put ideas into their heads, and they will do the rest. (VIII. 307)

Let us repeat this day and night, and say, "Nothing for me ; no matter whether the thing is good, bad, or indifferent ; I do not care for it ; I sacrifice all unto Thee." Day and night let us renounce our seeming self until it becomes a habit with us to do so, until it gets into the blood, the nerves, and the brain, and the whole body is every moment obedient to this idea of self-renunciation. (I. 102)

Let us say, "We are" and "God is" and "We are God", *"Shivoham, Shivoham",* and march on. (IV. 351)

Let us struggle for higher and better things ; look not back, no, not even if you see the dearest and nearest cry. (V. 10)

Let us work without desire for name or fame or rule over the others. Let us be free from the triple bonds of lust, greed of gain, and anger. (VIII. 350)

Let us worship the spirit in spirit, standing on spirit. Let the foundation be spirit, the middle spirit, the culmination spirit. (VIII. 120)

Let your life be as deep as the ocean, but let it also be as wide as the sky. (V. 227)

Let your position be always that of the giver ; give your love unto God, but do not ask anything in return even from Him. (III. 88)

Let your souls ascend day and night like an "unbroken string" unto the feet of the Beloved whose throne is in your own hearts and let the rest take care of themselves, that is the body and everything else. (VI. 262)

Light, bring light ; Let light come unto every one ; the task will not be finished till every one has reached the Lord. (III. 247)

Like rolling river free thou ever be. (IV. 395)

Live alone in your mind—that is happiness. (VIII. 414)

Live alone or in the company of holy ones. (VII. 90)

"Live alone, walk alone." (V. 72)

Live for an ideal, and leave no place in the mind for anything else. (II. 37)

Live in harmony with all. Give up all idea of egoism, and entertain no sectarian views. Useless wrangling is a great sin. (VI. 329)

Live in the midst of the battle of life. (VI. 84)

Look at the "ocean" and not at the "wave" ; see no difference between ant and angel. (VII. 7)

Look not at me, look to yourselves. (V. 51)

Look not for success or failure. Join yourself to the perfectly unselfish will and work on. (VI. 83)

Look not for the truth in any religion ; it is here in the human soul, the miracle of all miracles—in the human soul, the emporium of all knowledge, the mine of all existence—seek here. (I. 355)

Look upon every man, woman, and every one as God. You cannot help anyone, you can only serve : serve the children of the Lord, serve the Lord Himself, if you have the privilege. (III. 246)

Look within yourself and find the truth that you had (forgotten). (I. 500)

Lose regard for the body ; get rid of the consciousness of it so far as possible. (VII. 67)

Love all things only through and for the Self. (VII. 69)

Love and do good to everybody, but do not become a slave. (IV. 6)

Love and ask nothing ; love and look for nothing further. (VII. 29)

Love the poor, the miserable, the downtrodden, and the Lord will bless you. (V. 23)

Lower not your standard of purity, morality, and love of God. (VIII. 382)

M

Make a blaze ! Make a blaze ! (VI. 377)

Make it a rule not to eat until you have practised (Yoga) ; if you do this, the sheer force of hunger will break your laziness. (I. 145)

Make men first. (V. 333)

Make your life a manifestation of will strengthened by renunciation. (VIII. 227)

Make your nerves strong. What we want is muscles of iron and nerves of steel. (III. 224)

Make yourself a fit agent to work. (VIII. 223)

Make yourselves decent men ! ...Be chaste and pure ! ...There is no other way. (I. 520)

Men must have education. They speak of democracy, of the equality of all men, these days. But how will a man know he is equal with all ? (VIII. 94)

Man should hunger for one thing alone, the spirit, because spirit alone exists. (VIII. 119)

Manifest the divinity within you, and everything will be harmoniously arranged around it. (IV. 351)

March ahead, Children of the Aryans ! (III. 368)

Meditate whenever you get time. (VII. 267)

Mind your own Karma ; a load of Karma is there in you to work out. (III. 246)

My children should be brave, above all. (V. 264)

My disciples must not be cowards. (V. 87)

My old watchword—struggle, struggle up to light ! Onward ! (VI. 320)

N

Nature must fall at your feet and you must trample on it and be free and glorious by going beyond. (III. 128)

Neither money pays nor name, nor fame, nor learning ; it is character that can cleave through adamantine walls of difficulties. Bear this in mind. (VII. 487)

Neither seek nor avoid, take what comes. (VII. 14)

Never allow weakness to overtake your mind. (VII. 234)

Never be anxious for a moment. (VI. 261)

Never be weak. You must be strong ; you have infinite strength within you. (IV. 11)

Never fear what will become of you, depend on no one. (VII. 49)

Never forget this is only a momentary state, and that we have to pass through it. (I. 249)

Never lose faith in yourself, you can do anything in this universe. Never weaken, all power is yours. (VII. 85)

Never lose heart. In eating, dressing, or lying, in singing or playing, in enjoyment or disease, always manifest the highest moral courage. (VII. 233)

Never mistake hysterical trances for the real thing. (VII. 60)

Never pander to weakness. (VII. 79)

Never quarrel about religion. All quarrels and disputations concerning religion simply show that spirituality is not present. Religious quarrels are always over the husks. When purity, when spirituality goes, leaving the soul dry, quarrels begin, and not before. (VI. 127)

Never say man is weak. (VIII. 229)

Never say "mine". Whenever we say a thing is "mine", misery will immediately come. (I. 100)

Never say, "No", never say, "I cannot", for you are infinite. (II. 300)

Never say, "O Lord, I am a miserable sinner." (III. 26)

Never tell yourselves or others that you are weak. (II. 302)

Never think you can make the world better and happier. (VII. 102)

Never turn back to see the result of what you have done. (VII. 10)

No foolish talk now, but actual work. (V. 64)

No man, no nation, my son, can hate others and live. (V. 52)

No more weeping, but stand on your feet and be men. (III. 224)

No need of looking behind. FORWARD ! We want infinite energy, infinite zeal, infinite courage, and infinite patience, then only will great things be achieved. (VI. 384)

No one is greater : realise you are Brahman. (VII. 54)

No saying "nay", no negative thoughts ! Say "Yea, Yea". "*Soham, Soham*"—"I am He ! I am He !" (VI. 274)

"None can help you ; help yourself ; work out your own salvation." (IV. 136)

"Not I, but Thou"—say it, feel it, live it. (VII. 15)

"Nothing is baser than calling our brother a sinner." (VII. 418)

Now, do not talk ; work, work, work ! (V. 65)

Now the only way out is to listen to the words of the Lord in the Gita.

"क्लैव्यं मास्म गमः पार्थ—Yield not to unmanliness, O Partha."

"तस्मात्त्वमुत्तिष्ठ यशोलभस्व—Therefore do thou arise and acquire fame." (V. 453)

Now work, work, work ! (V. 61)

O

O hero, awake, and dream no more. (VIII. 432)

"O Thou Eternal Spirit, make us spiritual ; O Thou Eternal Strength, make us strong ; O Thou Mighty One, make us mighty. " (IV. 480)

O ye modern Hindus, de-hypnotise yourselves. The way to do that is found in your own sacred books. (III. 193)

Off with laziness. (VI. 267)

Offer everything you have unto the service of the Lord. (I. 443)

On and on, work, work, this is only the beginning. (VII. 486)

Once you have pledged your faith to a particular teacher, stick to him with all force. (VII. 411)

One must follow the path for which one is best suited ; but in this age special stress should be laid on Karma-Yoga. (V. 414)

Only be sincere ; and if you are sincere, says Vedantism, you are sure to be brought to the goal. (III. 537)

Only don't get attached. (IV. 96)

Only get your mind to cling to Him as far as you can. For then only the great magic of this world will break of itself. (VI. 482)

Only have faith. Do not look up to the so called rich and great ; do not care for the heartless intellectual writers, and their cold-blooded newspaper articles. Faith, sympathy—fiery faith and fiery sympathy ! Life is nothing, death is nothing, hunger nothing, cold nothing. Glory unto the Lord—march on, the Lord is our General. (V. 17)

Only know the truth and realise it. (II. 148)

One should raise the self by the self. (V. 147)

Onward and forward, my old watchword. (VI. 305)

Onward, brave souls, we will gain ! Organise and found societies and go to work, that is the only way. (V. 38)

Onward for ever! Sympathy for the poor, the down-trodden, even unto death—this is our motto. Onward, brave lads ! (V. 30)

Onward, my brave boys—money or no money—men or
no men ! Have you love ? Have you God ? Onward
and forward to the breach, you are irresistible.
(IV. 369)

Open the windows of your hearts to the clear light of truth,
and sit like children at the feet of those who know
what they are talking about—the sages of India.
(III. 44)

Open your eyes and see that as such it never existed.
(II. 147)

Our countrymen must remember that in things of the Spirit
we are the teachers, and not foreigners.
(V. 112)

Our first duty ought to be to look into our own souls and
find whether the craving in the heart is real. (III. 47)

Ours is to do good works in our lives and hold an example
before others. (VII. 221)

P

Pass from non-existence to existence, from darkness to
light. (VI. 91)

Perish in the struggle to be holy ; a thousand times
welcome death. (VI. 121)

Persevere. All progress proceeds by such rise and fall.
(I. 221)

Persevere on, my brave lads. We have only just begun.
Never despond ! Never say enough ! (V. 119)

Plant in your heart the faith of Nachiketa. (VI. 472)

Please be careful not to become impure even in thought, as also in speech and action ; always try to do good to others as far as in you lies. (VI. 246)

Please read the Gita everyday to the best of your opportunity. (VI. 247)

Plod on through the dark, brave heart, with all thy might and main. (IV. 390)

Plunge in ! Do the duty at hand. (IV. 131)

Plunge into the fire and bring the people towards the Lord. (V. 66)

Practise (Yoga) hard ; whether you live or die does not matter. You have to plunge in and work, without thinking of the result. (I. 178)

Practise truthfulness. Twelve years of absolute truthfulness in thought, word, and deed gives a man what he wills. (VI. 124)

Preach His name, let His teachings penetrate the world to the very bone. (VI. 411)

Preach, preach unto the world the great truths of your religion ; the world waits for them. (III. 224)

Preach the highest truths broadcast. (V. 264)

Proclaim at the top of thy voice: "The Indian is my brother, the Indian is my life. India's gods and goddesses are my God. India's society is the cradle of my infancy, the pleasure-garden of my youth, the sacred heaven, the Varanasi of my old age. (IV. 480)

Proclaim the glory of the Atman with the roar of a lion, and impart fearlessness unto all beings by saying, "Arise, awake and stop not till the goal is reached." (VII. 138)

Proclaim to the whole world with trumpet voice. "There is no sin in thee, there is no misery in thee ; thou art the reservoir of omnipotent power. Arise, awake, and manifest the Divinity within !" (IV. 110)

Purify yourself, and the world is bound to be purified. (I. 426)

Put God behind everything—man, animal, food, work ; make this a habit. (VII. 77)

Put out self, lose it, forget it ; just let God work, it is His business. (VII. 14)

Put your whole heart and soul in the work to which I have consecrated myself. (V. 383)

Put yourself to work, and you will find such tremendous power coming to you that you will feel it hard to bear. (V. 382)

R

Raise once more that mighty banner of Advaita, for on no other ground can you have that wonderful love until you see that the same Lord is present everywhere. (III. 430)

Reach a state where your very breathing is a prayer. (VII. 46)

Reach unity ; no more duality will come. (VII. 42)

Read man, he is the living poem. (VII. 89)

Realise in your own life this knowledge of Brahman which comprehends all theories and is the rationale of all truths, and preach it to the world. (VII. 197)

Realise religion, no talking will do. (II. 165)

Realise yourself. That is all there is to do. (IV. 246)

Reason out what is true from what is untrue. (VIII. 228)

Receive no gifts. (I. 260)

Relax your limbs and float with the current, and you are sure to reach your destination. (VI. 286)

Release the soul for ever. (IV. 395)

Religion, the common inheritance, the universal birthright of the race, must be brought free to the door of everybody. (III. 383)

Remain pure always. (VI. 246)

Remember, it is His will—I am a voice without a form. (VI. 283)

Remember Mahavira, remember the Divine Mother ! And you will see that all weakness, all cowardice will vanish at once. (VII. 234)

Remember, perfect devotion minus its bigotry—this is what we have got to show. (VI. 285)

Remember that perfect purity, disinterestedness, and obedience to the Guru are the secret of all success. (V. 111)

Remember that the nation lives in the cottage. (V. 29)

"Remember ! the message of India is always *'Not the soul for nature, but nature for the soul !'* (VIII. 261)

Remember the *only sign of life* is motion and growth. (V. 38)

Remember your great mission in life. (III. 443)

Remove the cloud and the sun will manifest. Then you get into the state of " भिद्यते हृदयग्रन्थिः"("the knot of the heart is broken") etc. (VI. 457)

Remove the veils of ignorance by purity, then we manifest ourselves as we really are and know that we were never in bondage. (VII. 103)

Renounce and be happy. (V. 138)

Renounce and give up. (II. 100)

Renounce everything. (I. 453)

Renounce the lower so that you may get the higher. (IV. 243)

Renunciation, renunciation and renunciation—let this be the one motto of your lives. (VI. 488)

Renunciation !—Renunciation !—You must preach this above everything else. (VI. 276)

Repeat and pray day and night, "O Thou Lord of Gauri, O Thou Mother of the Universe, vouchsafe manliness unto me ! O Thou Mother of Strength, take away my weakness, take away my unmanliness, and make me a man !" (IV. 480)

Resign everything unto God. In this tremendous fiery furnace where the fire of duty scorches everybody,

drink this cup of nectar and be happy. We are all
simply working out His will, and have nothing to do
with rewards and punishments. (I. 104)

Resist not evil. Face it! You are higher than evil.
(VIII. 111)

Resist not evil done to yourself, but you may resist evil
done to others. (VI. 119)

Reverse the current ; bring in the opposite vibration, and
behold the magic transformation ! (IV. 110)

Revile none. Even those customs that are now appearing
to be positive evils, have been positively life-giving in
times past ; and if we have to remove these, we must
not do so with curses, but with blessings and
gratitude for the glorious work these customs have
done for the preservation of our race.
(III. 175)

Rise thou effulgent one, rise thou who art always pure, rise
thou birthless and deathless, rise almighty, and
manifest thy true nature. (II. 357)

Root out priestcraft first. (V. 10)

"Root out selfishness, and everything that makes you
selfish." (IV. 131)

Rouse yourselves, therefore, or life is short. There are
greater works to be done than aspiring to become
lawyers and picking quarrels and such things.
(III. 304)

S

Save yourself by yourself. (V. 48)

Say, day and night, "Come up, my brothers ; You are the infinite ocean of purity ! Be God ! Manifest as God! (VIII. 228)

Say day and night, "Thou art my father, my mother, my husband, my love, my lord, my God—I want nothing but Thee, nothing but Thee, nothing but Thee. Thou in me, I in Thee, I am Thee. Thou art me". (VI. 262)

Say, "Everything is in me, and I can manifest it at will." (VI. 277)

Say, "I am the Spirit ! Nothing external can touch me." When evil thoughts arise, repeat that, give that sledge-hammer blow on their heads, "I am the Spirit! I am the Witness, the Ever-Blessed ! I have no reason to do, no reason to suffer, I have finished with everything, I am the Witness. I am in my picture gallery—this universe is my museum, I am looking at these successive paintings. They are all beautiful. Whether good or evil. I see the marvellous skill, but it is all one. Infinite flames of the Great Painter !" (V. 254)

Say not man is a sinner. Tell him that he is a God. Even if there were a devil, it would be our duty to remember God always, and not the devil. (IV. 351)

Say not that you are weak. The spirit is omnipotent. Look at that handful of young men called into existence by the divine touch of Ramakrishna's feet. (IV. 352)

Say, "The ignorant Indian, the poor and destitute Indian, the Brahmin Indian, the Pariah Indian, is my brother." (IV. 480)

Search truth for yourself ; realise it yourself. Then if you find it beneficial to one and many, give it to people. (VIII. 104)

See everything, do everything, but be not attached. As soon as extreme attachment comes, a man loses himself, he is no more master of himself, he is a slave. (IV. 6)

See God in everything and everywhere. (II. 151)

See God in man. (IV. 31)

See God in your children. (II. 146)

See Him in your own soul. That is practical religion. (IV. 246)

See only God in every man, woman and child ; see it by the *antarjyotis*, "inner light", and seeing that, we can see naught else. (VII. 63)

See that God alone is true. (VIII. 228)

Seek first the kingdom of Heaven, and let everything else go. (VII. 100)

Seek for the highest, aim at that highest and you *shall* reach the highest. (VI. 262)

"Seek no help from high or low, from above or below. Desire nothing—and look upon this vanishing panorama as a witness and let it pass." (VI. 300)

Seek no praise, no reward, for anything you do. (I. 104)

Seek not, and that is God. (V. 275)

Seek not, touch not with your toes even, anything that is uncanny. (VI. 262)

Seek the Highest, always the Highest, for in the Highest is eternal bliss. (V. 275)

Seek the Lord and the Lord only. (VII. 64)

Seek the science of the maker and not that of the made. (VII. 64)

Send a good thought for every being in the three worlds. (IV. 350)

Serve as worship of the Lord Himself in the poor, the miserable, the weak. (IV. 246)

Serve the living God ! God comes to you in the blind, in the halt, in the poor, in the weak, in the diabolical. (I. 442)

Set yourselves wholly to the service of others. (V. 330)

Sit in a straight posture. (I. 145)

"Slow but sure." (VII. 445)

So, do your work. (II. 149)

So long as you are pure, and true to your principles, you will never fail—Mother will never leave you, and all blessings will be yours. (V. 96-97)

"Some would call you a saint, some a *Chandala* ; some a lunatic, others a demon. Go on then straight to thy work without heeding either." (VII. 468)

Speak of this Atman to all, even to the lowest. (VII. 199-200)

Speak out the truth boldly. (V. 263)

Spread ideas—go from village to village, from door to door—then only there will be real work. (VI. 264)

Spread only what he (Sri Ramakrishna) came to teach. Never mind his name—it will spread of itself. (VI. 274)

Spread ! Spread ! Run like fire to all places. (VI. 267)

Stamp out the negative spirit as if it were a pestilence, and it will conduce to your welfare in every way. (VI. 276)

Stand and die in your own strength, if there is any sin in the world, it is weakness ; avoid all weakness, for weakness is sin, weakness is death. (III. 151)

Stand as a rock ; you are indestructible. (II. 236)

Stand as a witness, as a student, and observe the phenomena of nature. (III. 74)

Stand aside, and freely let these frictions come. You feel the frictions only when you are in the current of the world, but when you are outside of it simply as a witness and as a student, you will be able to see that there are millions and millions of channels in which God is manifesting Himself as Love. (III. 74)

Stand firm like a rock. (V. 57)

Stand in that reverent attitude to the whole universe, and then will come perfect non-attachment. (V. 246)

Stand in the whirl and madness of action and reach the Centre. (VI. 84)

Stand on your own feet, and assimilate what you can ; learn from every nation, take what is of use to you. (III. 152)

Stand on your own Self. (VII. 89)

Stand sane and motiveless. (III. 529)

Stand thou in the spirit ! That is the goal. (VIII. 120)

Stand up. (II. 403)

Stand up and die game ! ...Do not add one lunacy to another. Do not add your weakness to the evil that is going to come. (I. 479)

Stand up and express the divinity within you. (III. 284)

Stand up and reason out, having no blind faith. Religion is a question of being and becoming, not of believing. (IV. 216)

Stand up and say, I am the master, the master of all. We forge the chain, and we alone can break it. (VII. 54)

Stand up, assert yourself, proclaim the God within you, do not deny Him ! (III. 193)

Stand up, be bold, and take the blame on your own shoulders. (III. 429)

Stand up, be bold, be strong. Take the whole responsibility on your own shoulders, and know that you are the creator of your own destiny. All the strength and succour you want is within yourselves. (II. 225)

Stand up for God ; let the world go. (VII. 101)

Stand up, men and women, in this spirit, dare to believe in the Truth, dare to practise the Truth ! The world requires a few hundred bold men and women. Practise that boldness which dares know the Truth, which dares show the Truth in life, which does not

quake before death, nay, welcomes death, makes a
man know that he is the Spirit, that, in the whole
universe, nothing can kill him. (II. 85)

Stand up then and be free. Know that every thought and
word that weakens you in this world is the only evil
that exists. (II. 236)

Stand upon the Self, then only can we truly love the world.
(VII. 11)

Stand upon truth, and you have got God. (VII. 72)

Stick to truth and we shall succeed, maybe slowly, but
surely. (IV. 370)

Stick to your beliefs. (VII. 428)

Stick to your reason until you reach something higher ; and
you will know it to be higher, because it will not jar
with reason. (VII. 60)

Stop not to look back for name, or fame, or any such
nonsense. Throw self overboard and work. (V. 34)

Stretch forth a helping hand, and open the gates of
knowledge to one and all, and give the downtrodden
masses once more their just and legitimate rights and
privileges. (III. 461)

Strength, O man, strength, says the Upanishads, stand up
and be strong. (III. 237)

Strike off thy fetters ! (IV. 393)

Strive after that Rishihood, stop not till you have attained
the goal, and the whole world will of itself bow at
your feet ! (III. 457)

Struggle Godward ! Light must come. (IV. 127)

Struggle hard to get money, but don't get attached to it. (IV. 96)

Struggle on! (I. 501)

Struggle, still say I. (IV. 367)

Study, and then meditate on what you have studied. (I. 220)

Study everything, but keep your own seat firm. (I. 474)

T

Take care of these two things—love of power and jealousy. (V. 52)

Take care that you do not swerve an inch from the ideal. (VII. 233)

Take courage and work on. Patience and steady work— this is the only way. (V. 96)

Take heart and work. (V. 62)

Take help of nature. (VI. 130)

Take off all ideas of growth from your mind. (II. 228)

Take off the name and form, and whatever is reality is He. (III. 422)

Take one thing up and do it, and see the end of it, and before you have seen the end, do not give it up. (I. 177)

Take refuge in God, only so can we cross the desert of Maya. (VII. 68)

"Take thy shoes from off thy feet, for the place whereon thou standest is holy ground." (IV. 28)

Take up a great ideal and give up our whole life to it. (III. 304)

Take up an idea, devote yourself to it, struggle on in patience, and the sun will rise for you. (VI. 135)

Take up one idea. Make that one idea your life—think of it, dream of it, live on that idea. Let the brain, muscles, nerves, every part of your body, be full of that idea, and just leave every other idea alone. (I. 177)

Take up what suits you, and let others take up what they need. (II. 350)

Take your stand on good purpose, right means, righteous courage, and be brave. (V. 462)

Take yourself away from all the world's little selfish clingings. (III. 74)

Teach man of the strength that is already within them. (II. 300)

Teach the Godhood of man. (VII. 54)

Teach your children that they are divine, that religion is a positive something and not a negative nonsense ; that it is not subjection to groans when under oppression, but expansion and manifestation. (I. 330)

Teach yourselves, teach every one his real nature, call upon the sleeping soul and see how it awakes. (III. 193)

Tell each and all that infinite power resides within them, that they are sharers of immortal Bliss. (VII. 182)

Tell the truth boldly, whether it hurts or not. (VII. 79)

Tell this to everybody—"Have no fear." (VII. 136)

"Test everything, try everything, and then believe it, and if you find it for the good of many, give it to all." (III. 528)

Test your love and humility. (VI. 145)

That is the secret ; that non-attachment. Be the Witness. (V. 254)

"The basis of all religions is the same, wherever they are; try to help them all you can, teach them all you can, but do not try to injure them." (I. 391)

The country must be raised. (V. 389)

The Hindus must back their talk with real work. (V. 64)

The Lord is with you. Take heart ! (VI. 266)

The mind usually works in a circle ; make it remain on one point. (VI. 136)

The one vital duty incumbent on you, if you really love your religion, if you really love your country, is that you must struggle hard to be up and doing, with this one great idea of bringing out the treasures from your closed books and delivering them over to their rightful heirs. (III. 134)

The principle is eternal and must be there. Work it out afresh and make a re-formed application. (III. 409)

The reformers must be able to unite in themselves the culture of both the East and the West. (VIII. 308)

The whole world is full of the Lord. Open your eyes and see Him. (II. 146)

There is too much talk, talk, talk ! (V. 66)

There must not be the slightest divergence between one's words and actions. (VII. 251)

Therefore, children of the Aryans, do not sit idle ; awake, arise, and stop not till the goal is reached. (III. 428)

Therefore it is right for you that you should serve your millions of brothers rather than aggrandise this little self. (III. 446)

Think always, "I am Brahman". (III. 25)

Think always "*Soham, Soham*" ; this is almost as good as liberation. (VII. 38)

Think and meditate that you are the omnipresent Atman. (VII. 196)

Think away everything. (VI. 91)

Think of God all the time, and that will purify you (VII. 104)

Think of Him, speak of Him. (VI. 90)

"Think of Him, think of Him alone, and give up all other vain words." (III. 80)

Think of nothing but liberation. (VII. 92)

Think of your higher self, not of your lower. (I. 327)

Think some thought ; it doesn't matter whether you are right or wrong. But think something ! (IV. 127)

This idea of the body and of the mind must go, must be driven off. (III. 27)

This life is a hard fact; work your way through it boldly, though it may be adamantine ; no matter, the soul is stronger. (II. 182)

This rascal ego must be obliterated. Power to help mankind is with the silent ones who only live and love and withdraw their own personality entirely. (VIII. 31)

Those of you who are Sannyasins must try to do good to others, for Sannyasa means that. (III. 446)

Those that want to help mankind must take their own pleasure and pain, name and fame, and all sorts of interests, and make a bundle of them and throw them into the sea, and then come to the Lord. This is what all the Master *said* and *did*. (VI. 302)

Thou art omnipotent—go, go to the mouth of the cannon, fear not. (IV. 110)

Thou brave one, be bold, take courage, be proud that thou art an Indian, proudly proclaim, "I am an Indian, every Indian is my brother." (IV. 480)

Through the terrors of evil, say—my God, my love ! Through the pangs of death, say—my God, my love ! Through all the evils under the sun, say—my God, my love! (VI. 262)

Throw away all weakness. (I. 146)

Throw away everything, even your own salvation, and go and help others. (III. 431)

Throw overboard all idea of jealousy and egotism, once for all. (VI. 278)

Throw the ideas broadcast, and let the result take care of itself. (IV. 351)

Throw your religious observances overboard for the present and be first prepared for the struggle for existence. (VII. 145)

To be good, we have all to be merciful. Even justice and right should stand on mercy. (I. 59)

To love anyone personally is bondage. Love all alike, then all desires fall off. (VII. 66)

To understand a nation, you must first understand its ideal. (VIII. 55)

Train up a band of fiery young men. (V. 35)

Trample law under your feet. There is no law in human nature, there is no destiny, no fate. How can there be law in infinity ? Freedom is its watchword. (II. 323)

Truce to foolish talk ; talk of the Lord. Life is too short to be spent in talking about frauds and cranks. (V. 65)

Trust not to the so-called rich, they are more dead than alive. (V. 16)

Truth must triumph. (V. 55)

Try to be moral, try to be brave, try to be sympathising. (V. 3)

Try to expand. (V. 38)

Try to love anybody and everybody. (V. 3)

Turn from all and seek only God. (VIII. 37)

Turn thy gaze inward, where resides the Paramatman. (IV. 110)

U

Unfurl that banner of Love ! (III. 430)

Up boys, and put yourselves to the task ! (V. 32)

V

Vow, then, to devote your whole lives to the cause of the redemption of these three hundred millions, going down and down every day. (V. 17)

W

Wait and grow, and you attain everything. (I. 473)

Wait for the time to come. Do not hurry. (V. 45)

Wait, have patience, everything will come right in time. (V. 45)

"Wake up, stop not until the goal is reached." (V. 35)

Wait with patience and love and strength ; if helpers not ready now, they will come in time. Why should we be in hurry ? The real working force of all great work is in its almost unperceived beginnings. (IV. 279)

Want of sympathy and lack of energy are at the root of all misery, and you must therefore give these two up. (VI. 357)

Want only God, take nothing else, let not "seeming" cheat you any longer. (VIII. 37)

We are *azad* (free), we must realise it. (VII. 47)

We are here to work, and will have to leave all when the call comes. (V. 330)

We are to give up and not to take. (VII. 466)

We must all work incessantly. (I. 53)

We must be as broad as the skies, as deep as the ocean ; we must have the zeal of the fanatic, the depth of the mystic, and the width of the agnostic. (VI. 137)

We must be the masters, and not the slaves of nature ; neither body nor mind must be our master, nor must we forget that the body is mine, and not I the body's. (I. 140)

We must become thinkers. (VIII. 135)

We must electrify society, electrify the world. (VI. 293)

We must first have the strong desire to get free. (VII. 92)

We must get out of materialism. (VIII. 135)

We must go out, we must conquer the world through our spirituality and philosophy. There is no other alternative, we must do it or die. (III. 277)

We must look with perfect calmness upon all the *panorama* of the world. (VII. 11)

We must love God for love's sake, we must do our duty to Him for duty's sake, and must work for Him for work's sake and must worship Him for worship's sake. (II. 502)

We must not be attached. That is to say, we must not be drawn away from the work by anything else ; still, we must be able to quit the work whenever we like. (II. 2)

We must not hurt others. (VIII. 32)

We must not look down with contempt on others. All of us are going towards the same goal. The difference between weakness and strength is one of degree ; the difference between virtue and vice is one of degree ; the difference between heaven and hell is one of degree ; the difference between life and death is one of degree ; all differences in this world are of degree, and not of kind, because oneness is the secret of everything. (II. 299)

We must persevere until the goal is reached. (I. 259)

We must plunge heart and soul and body into the work. (VI. 301)

We must rouse India and the whole world. (V. 61-62)

We must set the whole world afire.(VIII. 353)

We must "sin" (that is, make mistakes) in order to rise to Godhood. (VIII. 18)

We must try our best to destroy ignorance and evil. Only we have to learn that evil is destroyed by the growth of good. (V. 125)

We shall have to work, giving up altogether all desire for results. People will call us both good and bad. But we shall have to work like lions, keeping the ideal before us, without caring whether "the wise ones praise or blame us". (VII. 231-32)

We should engage in such works as bring the largest amount of good and the smallest measure of evil. (V. 248)

Weep ! Weeping clears the eyes and brings about intuition. (IV. 492)

What fear is there ? (VII. 194)

What fear ! Whom to fear ! Steel your hearts and set yourselves to work ! (VI. 326)

What is there to fear ? Fear is death—fear is the greatest sin. (VII. 200)

What is wanted is practical sort of work. (II. 493)

What you want is character, strengthening of the will. (II. 357)

Whatever you do let that be your worship for the time. (V. 114)

When you have got the human body, then rouse the Atman within and say—I have reached the state of fearlessness. (VII. 213)

When you help a poor man, do not feel the least pride. That is worship for you, and not the cause of pride. (II. 237)

Whenever darkness comes, assert the reality and everything adverse must vanish. (II. 403)

We give thirsty people ditch-water to drink whilst the river of life and truth flows by ? (VII. 499)

Why look up to men for approbation, look up to God ! (VI. 338)

Woman ! thou shalt not be coupled with anything connected with the flesh. (VIII. 58)

Work as if on each of you depended the whole work.
   (IV. 370)

Work ! Be unattached ! That is the whole secret. (I. 442)

Work, but give up the results to the Lord. (VII. 38)

Work day and night ! (I. 441)

Work for the *idea*, not the person. (V. 68)

Work for them, love them, do good to them, sacrifice a
   hundred lives, if need be, for them, but never be
   attached. (IV. 96)

Work for work's sake. (I. 32)

"Work for work's sake. Worship for worship's sake. Do
   good because it is good to do good. Ask no more."
   (I. 456)

Work hard. Be holy and pure and the fire will come.
   (V. 38)

Work hard, be steady, and have faith in the Lord. (V. 29)

"Work incessantly, but give up all attachment to work."
   (I. 100)

Work incessantly, holding life as something deified, as God
   Himself, and knowing that, this is all we have to do,
   this is all we should ask for. (II. 150)

Work in harmony. (V. 61)

Work of your own free will, not from duty. (VII. 49)

Work on. (IV. 370)

Work on ; be lions ; and the Lord will bless you. I shall
   work incessantly until I die, and even after death I
   shall work for the good of the world. (V. 64)

Work on ! Hold on! Be brave ! Dare anything and
 everything. (V. 112)

Work on, the best way you can. (V. 106)

Work on—the Lord is behind the work. Mahashakti is with
 you. (V. 110)

Work on with a heart. (V. 124)

Work on with all energy. (V. 116)

Work on with the intrepidity of a lion but, at the same time
 with the tenderness of a flower. (V. 332)

Work out the salvation of this land and of the whole world,
 each of you thinking that the entire burden is on your
 shoulders. (III. 199)

Work out your own religion [salvation]. (VII. 430)

Work out your own salvation. (VII. 86 ; VII. 289 ;
 VIII. 105)

Work through freedom ! Work through love ! The word
 "love" is very difficult to understand ; love never
 comes until there is freedom. There is no true love
 possible in the slave. (I. 57)

Work to lift people ! (I. 441)

Work unto death—I am with you, and when I am gone, my
 spirit will work with you. (V. 114)

Work, work. (IV. 369)

Work, work—conquer all by your love ! (V. 38)

Work, work, for, to work only for the good of others is life.
 (IV. 369)

Work, work the idea, the plan, my boys, my brave, noble, good souls—to the wheel, to the wheel put your shoulders. (V. 34)

Work, work, work—let this be your motto. (VI. 278)

Worship everything as God—every form is His temple. (VIII. 136)

Worship God with Bhakti tempered with Jnana. (V. 347)

Worship Him who alone stands by us, whether we are doing good or are doing evil ; who never leaves us even ; as love never pulls down, as love knows no barter, no selfishness. (VI. 102)

Y

Yet have the power to give : give, and there it ends. Learn that the whole life is giving, that nature will force you to give. So, give willingly. (II. 5)

You do your own duty, and leave the rest to Him. (V. 78)

You are to see God in the wife. (II. 146)

You have the right to work, but do not become so degenerate as to look for results. (VI. 83-84)

You have to behold the Atman in this car of the body. (VII. 120)

You have to go beyond all fear. (VI. 473)

You have to grow from inside out. (V. 410)

You have to realise truth and work it out for yourself according to your own nature. (VI. 65)

You have to see God yourself. (I. 469)

You have to teach yourself ; your growth must come from inside. (II. 385)

You must all be free. (VI. 57)

You must all pay attention to your health first. (VI. 304)

You must be all-forbearing, like Mother Earth. (VI. 278)

You must be as free as the air, and as obedient as the plant and the dog. (III. 448)

You must be perfectly pure. Do not think of evil things, such thoughts will surely drag you down. (VI. 125)

You must be ready to plunge into fire—then will work be done. (VI. 322)

You must be Rishis yourselves. (III. 447)

You must come out from all form if you would see the Light. (VI. 82)

You must end where you begin ; and as you began in God, you must go back to God. (IV. 215-16)

You must expand if you want to live. The moment you have ceased to expand, death is upon you, danger is ahead. (III. 272)

You must express your sympathy with people of all sects. (VI. 305)

You must give your body, mind, and speech to "the welfare of the world." (VI. 288)

You must have a great devotion to your ideal, devotion not of the moment, but calm, persevering, and steady devotion, like that of a Chataka (a kind of bird) which looks into the sky in the midst of thunder and lightning and would drink no water but from the clouds. (VI. 121)

You must have a hold on the masses. (V. 36)

You must have an iron will if you would cross the ocean. You must be strong enough to pierce mountains. (VI.297)

You must have strict morality. Deviate an inch from this, and you are gone for ever. (VII. 447)

You must hold fast and be steady in the search for truth. (VII. 31)

You must keep the mind fixed on one object, like an unbroken stream of oil. (VII. 253)

You must learn calm submission to the will of God. (VI. 118)

You must liberate the whole universe before you leave this body. (VII. 163)

You must not criticise others ; you must criticise *yourself.* (VI. 129)

You must not mistake *sattva* for dullness or laziness. (I. 202)

You must not say that you are weak. How do you know what possibilities lie behind that degradation on the surface ? (II. 302)

You must open your heart. (III. 283)

You must see God. The spirit must be realized, and that is practical religion. (IV. 246)

You must take off your mind from lust and lucre, must discriminate always between the real and the unreal—must settle down into the mood of bodilessness with the brooding thought that you are not this body, and must always have the realisation that you are the all-pervading Atman. (VI. 482)

You must worship the self in Krishna, not Krishna as Krishna. (VII. 57)

You should go to the sinking millions of India, and take them by the hand. (III. 433)

You, poor men of Bengal, come up, you can do everything, and you must do everything. (III. 445)

You should never try to follow another's path, for that is his way, not yours. (VI. 99)

You should work like a master and not as a slave ; work incessantly, but do not do slave's work. (I. 57)

Your country requires heroes ; be heroes ! (V. 51)

Your duty is to go on working, and then everything will follow of itself. (VII. 247)

Your way is the best for you, but that is no sign that it is the best for others. (VI. 99)

Your work is to serve the poor and miserable, without distinction of caste or colour. (VII. 247)

———